6⁵⁰

A CRY LIKE A BELL

A Cry
Like a Bell

Madeleine L'Engle

Harold Shaw Publishers
Wheaton, Illinois

The following poems first appeared in *The Weather of
the Heart* by Madeleine L'Engle, © Crosswicks, 1978,
and are reprinted and/or adapted by permission of
Harold Shaw Publishers:
"Jacob: ballade"
"O Simplicitas"
"O Sapientia"
"Like every newborn"
"Moses: dialogue with God"
"Temper my intemperance"

Grateful acknowledgment is made to Harper & Row,
Publishers, Inc. for the use of the poems "Pharaoh's
cross," "David," "After annunciation," "Mary speaks,"
"Mary speaks: from Ephesus" from *The Irrational Season*
by Madeleine L'Engle. Copyright © 1977 by Cross-
wicks, Ltd. Reprinted and adapted by permission of
Harper & Row, Publishers, Inc.

ISBN 0-87788-148-0

Cover photo: Luci Shaw

Library of Congress Cataloging-in-Publication Data

L'Engle, Madeleine.
    A cry like a bell: poems / by Madeleine L'Engle.
        p. cm. — (Wheaton literary series)
    ISBN 0-87788-148-0: $8.95
    1. Bible—History of Biblical events—Poetry.   2.
Christian poetry, American.   I. Title.   II. Series.
PS3523.E55C7 1987
811'.54—dc19   87-26940
                                                    CIP

96
10   9   8   7   6

for Madeleine Saunders Jones

Contents

A Fore Word

In this new volume of poetry, Madeleine L'Engle clothes herself in characters of the Bible and speaks through their mouths. The result is a remarkable series of personality studies in poetic form, in which men and women of the Old and New Testaments (and one beast—Balaam's ass) call to us in their authentic voices.

We learn how they are like us, and also how unlike. They are like us because they are human, and their struggles and dilemmas, their moments of ecstasy, and their heart-longings for God echo our own. We can be one with them, because they respond to the Creator much as we do—sometimes with zest, but often with reluctance and the sense of inadequacy to the challenge which the call of God awakes in all of us. And yet God was able to use his most unlikely children, unqualified, unloveable often, complicated and full of conflict, to be his representatives in the world.

They are unlike us because they seem to be in more direct contact with Jehovah than we, either through dreams and visions, or in direct speech with the Almighty, terrifying as that often was. Their times were more primitive, their responses more primal and direct than our own.

What is appealing about this series of poems, apart from the strength and skill of their author's art, is that there are no cardboard figures here, no conventional portraits, no individuals who seem impossibly pious or submissive or holy, and therefore removed from us.

Isaac says: "From now on, no fathers are to be trusted," and we learn why he felt like that.

Leah tells us: "We lived by deceit, all of us, one no better than the other . . . ," and we see her compliance with her father's plan in a new light.

One of the Wise Men murmurs, "I shall miss the stars," and we feel the paradoxical pain that the Light of Christ may cause as a new way of knowing is learned.

One of the most extraordinary of these poems comes from the mouth of the High Priest's servant, who has kept the ear that Peter severed from his head, and handles it, now "like a piece of fungus," reminding him of the enormous difference in him—"My life was shattered, turned around, changed forever" by the Man who healed him in that traumatic incident.

And Thomas: "As you depended from a tree,/so depend I, Lord, on thee . . . Thy limbs hold me, heal me, mend/all unbelieving doubts. . . ." and we find a new strength to cling to in our own times of unbelief.

Some of the most moving poems in this collection come through Mary's voice, in which we can hear her beautiful humanity and complexity.

In the words of Madeleine L'Engle, the dead come to life. Plangent as bells, with the urgency of blood speaking from the ground, these cries of pain and joy ring down the cycles of centuries, and listening to them, we are joined to their music.

Luci Shaw

Eve

When we left the garden we knew that it would be forever.
The new world we entered was dark and strange. Nights were cold.
We lay together for warmth, and because we were afraid
of the un-named animals, and of the others: we had never
known about the giants, and angels gone wild. We had not been told
of dwarves and elves; they teased us; we hid whenever they played.

Adam held me. When my belly grew taut and began to swell
I didn't know what was happening. I thought it was the beginning
of death, the very first death. I clung to Adam and cried.
As I grew bigger something within me moved. One day I fell
and the pains started. A true angel came and pushed the grinning
creatures back. Adam helped. There was a tearing. I thought I'd died.

Instead, from within me came a tiny thing, a new creature,
red-faced, bellowing, mouth groping for my breast.
This was not death, but birth, and joy came to my heart again.
This was the first-born child. How I did laugh and sing!
But from this birth came death. He never gave me any rest.
And then he killed his brother. Oh, my child. Oh, my son Cain.

I watched from then on over every birth,
seeing in each babe cruelty ready to kill compassion.
For centuries the pattern did not change. Birth always meant death.
Each manchild who was born upon the longing earth
in gratefulness and joy brought me only a fresh ration
of tears. I had let hate into the world with that first breath.

Yet something made me hope. Each baby born
brought me hurrying, bringing, as in the old tales, a gift

1

looking—for what? I went to every slum and cave and palace
seeking the mothers, thinking that at least I could warn
their hearts. Thus perhaps the balance might shift
and kindness and concern replace self-will and malice.

So I was waiting at that extraordinary intersection
of Eternity and Time when David's son (Adam's, too)
was born. I watched the Incarnate at his mother's breast
making, by his humble, holy birth the one possible correction
of all that I by disobedience had done. I knelt and saw new
Adam, and I cried, "My son!" and came at last to rest.

And God heard the voice of the lad (Ishmael), and the angel of God called to Hagar out of heaven, and said unto her, What aileth thee, Hagar? Fear not; for God hath heard the voice of the lad where he is.

And God opened her eyes, and she saw a fountain of water.
Genesis 21:17-19

Light
eye-thirsting for light
oh come
sight-drenching
night-wrenching
cloud-clearing
fountains of light
refreshing
renewing
caressing
blessing
star-flashing
love-revealing
dark blind-healing
day-dealing
eye-drenching
thirst-quenching
draughts of in-sight
in-light
eye
thy satellite
cloud-clearing
sun-searing
fear's flight
I

3

hearing
revering
adoring
thy
glory-splashing
light-crashing
Thee-light
O delight
O joy of thy
unextinguished
incomprehensible
glory of
light.

Sarah: before Mount Moriah

Like a small mouse
I am being played with.
Pushed around, sent from home,
passed off as a sister,
free to be the sport of others
(nobody asked me).
Nobody asked if I wanted
to leave home and all my friends
(the cat never asks the mouse).
Would my womb have filled
if we had stayed where we were
instead of following strange promises?
My maid, giving my husband a child for me,
then made mock of me.
So when the angel came
announcing—promising—
a child in my womb long dry
what could I do but laugh?
And then warmth came again, and fullness,
and my child was born,
my laughter, my joy.

But do not play with me any more!
What kind of logic lurks in your promise
that the sky full of stars
is like the number of our descendents
and then demand the son's life who makes
that promise possible?
Can I trust a breaker of promises?
What kind of game is this?

Are you laughing at my pain
as I watch the child and his father
climb the mountain?
Am I no more than a mouse
to be played with?

I am a woman.
You—father-God—
have yet to learn
what it is to be a mother,

and so, perhaps, have I.
And if you give me back my laughter again,
then, together we can learn
and I will say—oh, I will sing!—
that you have regarded the lowliness
of your handmaiden.

Abraham: with laughter

Unlike the other gods
you are not satisfied with holocausts
and the sweet smell of smoke.
Unlike the other gods
you do not let us be
but come and pitch your tent
with ours and sniff out
all we do. You are not satisfied
to have us satisfied,
to leave well enough alone.

No, you sent me out,
an old man, with your interfering
and your promises, and all your countings
of the stars and my son's son's sons.
You might have picked a better man
to fall before the terror of great darkness.
Twice, fear for my life
passed my wife off as sister.
Why not, with her barren womb?

And then a son. In my old age a son.
You do nothing like the other gods
and so I know you are my God
and my son's God and my son's sons'.
I do not understand the stars
uncountable in number;
nor do I understand you.

I wept. And when,
after all, you did not accept my sacrifice,
the ram brought laughter home.

The ram: caught in the bush

Asked to leave Eden
where I, with all the other beasts,
remained after the two-legged creatures left,
I moved to the gates and the cherub
with the flaming sword
drew aside to let me by, wings folded across his eyes.

I trotted along a path through woods,
across a desert, made a long detour
around a lake, and finally climbed
a mountain, till
the trees gave way to bushes
and a rock.
An old man raised a knife.

He stood there by the rock
and wept and raised his knife.
So these are men, I thought,
and shook my head in horror, and was caught
within the springing branches of a bush.
Then there was lightning,
and the thunder came,
and a voice cried out to me:
O my son, my son,
slain before the foundation
of the world.

I felt the knife's edge.
For this I came from Eden,
for my will is ever his,

as I am his, and have life
in him, and he in me.
Thus the knife pierced his own heart.

And the old man laughed with joy.

Isaac

From now on, no fathers are to be trusted.
I know.
I felt the knife at my throat before the angel
stopped my father's hand.

How did it come to that?
The three day journey to Mount Moriah
  and the sharpened blade
  and I, laid on the stone slab,
  prepared for sacrifice?
I, the great gift of my parents' old age,
  so unexpected as to cause them laughter,
  and then, when the miracle came,
  to bring them laughter,
  to be laughter, Isaac, I—
What kind of God the Father would ask Abraham,
  Abraham, his son,
  to offer up Isaac, his son.
  Why ask?
  Why demand obedience for such a wanton sacrifice?
How can my father's Father be a God of love?
How could my father sharpen the knife?

No, fathers are not to be trusted.

And when my father's Father
  sent his Son up the mountain for an offering
  who, then, demanded such a sacrifice?
  Who was it he obeyed

who sent no angel
and no ram?
Who was the father of my father's Father?

But, my father said, there is no Father's father.

Isaac: my very name means laughter,
    and I know only tears.

Would I laugh
if I could understand
that my father's Father
and the Son
and the ram caught by the horns
are one?

Esau

Wives I had already,
for no one (as usual) thought to guide me.
But my father, who gave my brother
the blessing which, like the birthright,
should have been mine,
told this favoured, cheating son
that the daughters of Canaan
were not good enough for him.
Ha! thought I, and went to Ishmael,
another first-born favoured by neither man nor God
and took his daughter to my wife and to my bed.

Mahaloth
who put a song in my heart
may God hear
and by my name
and the name of Mahaloth's father
and the well of water which God
gave him in the desert
I will sing my song to Mahaloth in
silence.

The world knows of Jacob's love
for Rachel,
and of God's love for Jacob
who took all which by birth was mine.
(My heel still hurts.)

But in Mahaloth
a fountain in the desert is mine
and a song in my heart
which God (if he wills)
may hear.

Rachel: at Joseph's birth

First
before babe's birth
is death
death to safety
to the womb's wondrous warmth
death to dear darkness

danger
terror of tidal wave
a cruelty of light
an agony of air
a push of breath invading
listless lungs

Cry, sweet son, rage
at the indignity of birth
at death to safety
(and death of your mother's shame).

Be born, child,
into this brilliant, dangerous world
where love's piercing light
perfects darkness

where love's light
through all our deaths
shines us into birth.

Rachel: birthing Benjamin

Fight the darkness. Fight.
Let night not rise.
Push the shadows back
with tearless eyes.
Fight the darkness. Bright
is the loving heart
pierced by the sword of light,
thrusting the darkness back.
Let night not rise.
Fight the darkness. Start
the fear-filled fight.
Love is the one surprise
that startles the dark.
Heed not the certain pain.
Hold anger back.
Push the shadows apart.
Dark's loss, light's gain,
fight the darkness, fight,
let it not rise.
Nor fear the pain.
Follow the light
which cannot be understood.
Oh break, my heart,
fight the darkness. Fight.
But O my God I would
push the shadows back
until I see the child.
Love is the one surprise.
I struggle toward the bright
joy that ends the night.

Benjamin's birth

Birth and death
the opening of new life
the first tentative breath
followed by the unwelcome knife
of death.

I heard the cry
resentful and rebellious
of my newborn son
reluctant to emerge
from the safe darkness
of the womb
darker perhaps
and further from life
than the unknown terror
of the tomb.

In the dark waters, the child
knows nothing of Time—
knows nothing of the time
when he will be propelled
from the dark into light
when life will begin
with pain and terror
and the responsibility of breath.
Is it better never to know birth?
Better than the sharp
knowledge of death?

Leah

We lived by deceit,
all of us,
one no better than the other,
I as bad as the rest,
willing to take my sister's place
in Jacob's bed on her wedding night—
humiliated, but still willing.

How could it be that Jacob did not know?
After a wedding feast such as Laban
gave his son-to-be
how could it not be?
And I loved him,
his strange, smooth body,
and his strong and joyous play.
Out of my love I bore him children,
left off bearing,
and bore again,
still unloved by him.
And when he had her, too, to wife
his god, or ours, or both,
closed my sister's womb,
and then, incomprehensible,
re-opened it.

My father, keeping our Jacob with us
by deceit, by deceit
was himself cheated,
Jacob taking
the best of his beasts.

Until, surprised at Laban's anger, he stole us
and we fled. Deceitful still,
my sister stole our father's gods
and sat on them.

And yet, from our deceit
and from our love
we gave to Jacob
twelve sons, twelve nations
and, in the end,
one God.

Leah: the unloved

Acceptance without hope is stark and cold,
slowing the warm beating of the heart
in a waterless desert. I am told
the teraphim will balance out each part:
"I gave you sons; I will not give you this;
this good I'll balance with this pain-filled evil.
After love's hope, another gets the kiss."
Laban's gods juggle — savage, and primeval.
My sons he loves; that is my only good.
Another hope is found in each hope's death.
Hope will not die; would that it could,
but back it comes with each expectant breath.
Unloved as I am, but love still tries to lift
acceptance into my heart's acceptable gift.

Jacob: ballade

Mortal and angel wrestle through the night,
Jacob struggling, wildly wondering why
an angel should choose man for this strange fight.
The crystal ladder breaks the fragile sky
as angels watch the two throughout the dark.
At dawn the angel smites tired Jacob's thigh;
forever will he bear the wound and mark
God's messenger has left him. And the light
of all the watching angels rises high;
the crystal ladder breaks the fragile sky.
The world is hushed and still; the earth is stark,
astonished at the angel's choice and Jacob's cry.
Forever will he wear the wound and mark
the Lord has left to show his humble might.
All those who wrestle thus must surely die
to live once more to show the wound's strange sight.
The crystal ladder breaks the fragile sky
as angels rise and fall. The singing lark
heralds the wild sun's brightly rising eye.
Forever will he bear the wound and mark.

Worn Jacob limps to show that God passed by;
(the crystal ladder breaks the fragile sky
and light shines bright within the glowing dark)
forever will he bear the wound and mark.

Jacob: after Rachel's death

She lay between me and the sleeping skins,
her body white, pliant, mine
to enter, to be enclosed by her withinness.
She lay between me and the sleeping skins.

The baby fills the empty air with cries.
The ground is red with lost blood.

She lay between me and the blowing sand,
brought by the hot east wind
that stings the skin like insects.
We held each other in the embrace
of wind—I was in her and she held me
close
like no other woman.
She lay between me and the stinging sand.

The baby cries . . .

She lay between me and approaching death,
between me and my brother's anger,
between me and the angel's steel-soft wings.
Her softness was my strength,
her willingness my courage.
How will I face the angel?

It is I who must care now
for the child.

Pharaoh's cross

It would be easier to be an atheist; it is the simple way out.
But each time I turn toward that wide and welcoming door
it slams in my face, and I—like my forbears—Adam, Eve—
am left outside the garden of reason and limited, chill science
and the arguments of intellect.
Who is this wild cherubim who whirls the flaming sword
'twixt the door to the house of atheism and me?

Sometimes in the groping dark of my not knowing
I am exhausted with the struggle to believe in you, O God.
Your ways are not our ways. Your ways are extraordinary.
You sent evil angels to the Egyptians and killed;
you killed countless babes in order that Pharaoh,
whose heart was hardened by you (that worries me, Lord)
might be slow to let the Hebrew children go.
You turned back the waters of the Red Sea
and your Chosen People went through on dry land
and the Egyptians were drowned, men with wives and children,
young men with mothers and fathers (your ways are not our ways)
and there was much rejoicing at all this death,
and the angels laughed and sang, and you stopped them, saying,
"How can you sing when my children are drowning?"

When your people reach Mount Sinai you warned Moses
not to let any of them near you lest you break forth
on them with death in your hand.
You are Love, and you command us to love,
and yet you yourself turn men's hearts to evil,
and you wipe out nations with one sweep of the hand—
the Amorites and the Hittites and the Peruzzites—

gone, all gone. It seems that any means will do, and yet—
all these things are but stories told about you by fallen man,
part of the story (for your ways are not our ways)
but not the whole story. You are our author,
and we try to listen and set down what you say,
but we suffer from faulty hearing and loss of language
and we get the words wrong.

Listen: you came to us as one of us
and lived with us and died for us and descended into hell for us
and burst out into life for us:

Do you now hold Pharaoh in your arms?

Moses

Where are you?
Are you?
Are you not-ness
Are you the terror of the loss of all senses
all sense
?

For us finite, fallen
spacebound, time enclosed beings—
it is not meet for us to come too close
(take off your sandals)
or try to comprehend
you
who are infinite
eternal, freely comprehending, comprehensive
therefore (if you will) beyond our rationality
demolishing all our reasonings
overturning all our fragile buildings
demolishing all structures where we look to see
you

and then you turn your back on us.

Perhaps
we come closest to you only thus
in your absence.

Put me in a cleft of the rock
protect me with your infinite hand
as the absolute silence

in the heart of the hurricane
shows me the sound of your footsteps.
And you, turning your back that I not be destroyed
may (if you will)
pass by.

Moses: dialogue with God

Come.

    When?

Now. This way. I will guide you.

    Wait! Not so fast.

Hurry. You. I said you.

    Who am I?

Certainly I will be with thee.

    Is nothing, then, what it is? I had rather the rod had
    stayed a rod and not become a serpent.

Come. Quickly. While the blast of my breath opens the sea.

    Stop. I'm thirsty.

Drink water from this rock.

    But the rock moves on before us.

Go with it and drink.

    I'm tired. Can't you stop for a while?

You have already tarried too long.

    But if I am to follow you I must know your name.

I will be that I will be.

    You have set the mountain on fire.

Come. Climb.

    I will be lost in the terror of your cloud.

You are stiff-necked and of a stiff-necked people.

    YOUR people, Lord.

Indubitably.

    Your wrath waxes hot. I burn.

Thus to become great.

    Show me, then, thy glory.

*No man may see my face and live. But I will cover you with
my hand while I pass by.*

My people will turn away and cry because the skin of my face
shines.
Did you not expect this?
I cannot enter the tent of the congregation while your
cloud covers it and your glory fills the tabernacle. Look.
It moves before us again. Can you not stay still?
Come. Follow.
But this river is death. The waters are dark and deep.
Swim.
Now will I see your face? Where are you taking me now?
Up the mountain with me before I die.
But death
bursts into light.
The death is
what it will be.
These men: they want to keep us here in three
tabernacles. But the cloud moves. The water springs
from a rock that journeys on.
You are contained in me.
But how can we contain you in ark or tabernacle or—
You cannot.
Where, then?
In your heart. Come.
Still?
I will be with thee.
Who am I?
You are that I will be. Come.

Gershom: son of Moses

Time and memory are rock under our feet.
But the rock journeys on,
higher than we, leading us
to the rock on which to build,
strangely giving wondrous water
for all our searing thirsts.

Time and memory are the rock
of ages breaking human time
sending down roots,
memories deeper than all our living
roots drinking the living waters
healing
blessing
redeeming all forgetfulness and folly
of time's trappings.

Time and memory are the rock
on which we stand and love and live
and know more than we know,
share more than we dare,
give more than we have
because the rock journeys us
toward wherever Love wills.

From the Lord's rock
comes radiant timeless joy.

Balaam's ass

Least important of all animals, I am a beast
of burden. I can carry heavy loads
and I am more patient than a camel,
gentler of nature, though occasionally stubborn.
I am not considered particularly intelligent,
and my name is used as an insult.
"He's an ass," someone will say with great contempt.

But when I see an angel in my path
I recognize a messenger of God.
"Stop!" the angel said to me, and so I stopped,
obeying God, rather than my master, Baalam,
who hit me and cursed me and did not see
the angel's brilliance barring our way.

Later, I took the path to Bethlehem
bearing God's bearer on my weary back,
and stood beside her in the stable,
sharing her pain, her loneliness, and then the joy.

I carried on my back the Lord himself,
riding, triumphant, into Jerusalem,
and all the crowd cried, *Hosannah!* and blessing!

But the blessing turned into a curse,
Hosanna into Crucify him! *Crucify him!*

Least important of all animals, beast of burden,
my heaviest burden is to turn the curse into a blessing,
to see the angel in my path
and to bear forever the blessing of my Lord.

Jepthah's daughter

Does anybody hear me? El! Are you there?
Where are you? You said you would always care.
If you are not, then there is nothing anywhere.

I call, I cry, against my fate I batter.
Sharp in my ears the echoes fall and shatter.
My father's vow is final. Does it matter

he never thought he'd see me first? His word
is final. Lord, you who know each animal, each bird—
if I speak softly, will I then be heard?

No. Hush. I make no sound at all.
I wait in silence, still, in case you call.
All barriers of self and will must fall.

Take me beyond the grasp of nights and days.
Death leads me on to neither time, nor place.
Even in the dark can come El's grace.

Oh, God. Oh, El. The darkness, El, the cold
between the stars. There's nothing here to hold.

So am I dead? This endless silence roars
and flings me with the tide on golden shores.

Who is this man, here, eating fish, and bread?
How can I see and hear him, being dead?

He hands me broken bread and I am broken.
I do not understand the word that he has spoken.

But he is waiting for me, bright as a star.
"It's all right, child," he says. "You are. You *are.*"

Jepthah's daughter, 2

All the things that I must leave are good
because you made them. In those first new days
when nothing something was and stars were glad
and matter blazed into a song of praise
you saw what you had made and called it good.

So why must I turn now from all these things?
Take leave of taste and sound and scent and sight?
I do not understand such alterings,
my father's promise made to bring me night.
El, let me feel the touch of angels' wings!

Farewell, farewell, though you do not forget
you made and called them good, all these that I
must leave. In a fair fragrant garden plot
did we betray what you had done, so die
because we turned away and thus forgot?

So we forget again and yet again,
born with decay like marrow in our bones.
Is honorable death done for your gain?
How can we all be what we were once?
How can we wash away the mortal stain?

Farewell, O desert sand and burning sun,
farewell, O wondrous sound of wind and song,
farewell, O living taste of bread and wine,

and touch of hand to hand within the throng.
Farewell to all that I have thought was mine.

Farewell to everything I thought was me
that I may know what these were meant to be.

Naaman, the leper

O all ye little gods of Baal
whose altars crown the highest places,
at whom I scream to no avail,
who greet me with a thousand faces

their promises false—these alien priests.
My stricken skin's a leper's still.
I gave them jewels, spread them feasts,
and yet they never have their fill.

O all ye little gods of Baal,
first I must call you each by name;
and hunt each one through hill and dale
who spread abroad their worthless claim.

O all ye little gods of fear,
in alien dark, in the unknown,
gods of the soft, self-pitying tear,
gods of the self-willed need to own,

O all ye golden gods of pride,
ye whining gods of sly self-will,
in the high places you abide
and I must come and hunt and kill.

Where are your priests to feel my sword?
Come, you seducers, come you all,
beneath the double-edged word
clay feet shall shatter, heads shall fall.

Ye gods of jealousy and greed,
of lazy lust, of tired minds bored,
of cold, hard hearts. How fast you breed
to keep me from the only Lord.

O gods who tempted my false pride.
That seven washings in the river
were far too easy! "Master, bide,
obey the prophet." Healed flesh does quiver.

O all ye little gods of Baal
in the high places of the land
if I should hunt you down and fail
Elijah's here to guide my hand.

David: from Psalm 32

Teach me to obey willingly,
turning at the word of your command.
Under strong touch of your hand,
help to obey lovingly,
not questioning the turn in the road,
needing neither spur nor goad,
following your word joyfully.

Lend me, Lord, your understanding
not like horse or stubborn mule
balking against your rule
without the whip of your commanding.

Merrily, Lord, help me to play,
ride me without bit or bridle,
ride me bareback, without saddle,
ride me, move me to obey.

David

Your altar smelled of the slaughter house.
The innocent eyes of tender beasts
lost in confusions of laws and vows
were the high price paid to you for feasts.
They had to be men of iron, your priests.

And so did I, born but to sing,
to tend the lambs and not to kill.
Why, my Lord, did you have to bring
me down from the safety of my hill
into the danger of your will?

I learned to fight, I learned to sin,
I battled heathen, fought with lust;
when you were on my side I'd win.
My appetites I could not trust.
I only knew your wrath was just.

What I desired I went and stole.
I had to fight against my son.
You bound my wounds and made me whole
despite the wrong that I had done.
I turned from you and tried to run.

You took me, also, by the hair
and brought me back before your altar.
You terrified me with your care.
Against your rage I could but falter.
You changed me, but refused to alter.

So I grew old, but there remained
within me still the singing boy.
I stripped and sang. My wife complained.
Yet all my ill did I destroy
dancing before you in our joy.

My God, my God, is it not meet
that I should sing and shout and roar,
leap to your ark with loving feet?
I praise thee, hallow, and adore,
and play before thee evermore.

David: after Psalm 49

Death my shepherd
my loneliness
leading me through dark pastures
into unknown, unknowable emptiness
death my shepherd
the other side of light
the no of God
death the Son
thy sun
beyond all consolation
past human touch
death my loneliness
aloneness
teach me this dark lyric for my harp
that I may sing.

Psalm 55:12-14: A contemplation of David

My heart is disquieted within me, and the fear of death
has fallen upon me, death of hope,
death of love, death of light,
for it is not an open enemy who has done me this dishonour,
for then I could have borne it;
(dark from dark is never a surprise;
hate where there is always hate is bitter, but bearable)
but it was thou, my guide, my old familiar friend,
who taught me the way, who kept my candle alight
(Were you only playing with matches?).
We took sweet counsel together,
and walked in this house of God as friends.
Then suddenly your words rained fire
and I could not escape the stormy wind and tempest.
Oh, my friend, you had hands and held me,
you had eyes and saw me; ears and heard me;
you had a mouth and spoke gently to me,
but now all I see is a painted wooden idol,
blind and deaf and dumb and unincarnate.
(Was it I who daubed flesh and blood
to this thing of clay?)

I brought you a cup of water; you dashed it to the floor.
I am emptied, and cold.

Sand stretches before me, and the desert is dark;
for company I find only my bare and broken bones.
My tears are my meat day and night.

O Light of the world, how do I rejoice?

Herman the Ezragite: Psalm 88:18

My lovers and friends hast thou put away from me, and hid mine
acquaintance out of my sight.

My friends are taken, and my love:
my heart is shaken,
    I move in loneliness into the cold,
hoarfrost beneath, ice stars above.
    My heart grows still: so grow I old.

Groping with empty hands I vow
soliloquies I'll not allow
    in this strange, frozen solitude
lest I should with weak tears endow
    the winter's breath, black, bleak, and rude.

The panic clang of closing doors
slams noisily into my prayers.
    I see the shut doors of the past,
their faces blank (tell me: who cares?).
    The future's doors are slamming fast.

If I should cry or weep or moan
I make myself the more alone.
    By laughter, only, and by jest
this fearfulness may be undone
    and I in loneliness find rest.

In doorless places I must go
step barefoot through the falling snow,
    followed or following, must not flee.
I cannot know nor seek to know
    where the next open place will be.

Annunciation

Sorrowfully
the angel appeared
before the young woman
feared
to ask what must be asked,
a task
almost too great to bear.
With care,
mournfully,
the angel bare
the tidings of great joy,
and then
great grief.
Behold, thou shalt conceive.
Thou shalt bring forth a son.
This must be done.
There will be no reprieve.

2

Another boy
born of woman (who shall also grieve)
full of grace
and innocence
and no offence—
a lovely one
of pure and unmarked face.

3

How much can a woman bear?

4

Pain will endure for a night
but joy comes in the morning.

His name is Judas.

That the prophets may be fulfilled
he must play his part.
It must be done.
Pain will endure.
Joy comes in the morning.

Bearer of love

The great swan's wings were wild as he flew down;
Leda was almost smothered in his embrace.
His crimson beak slashed fiercely at her gown—
lust deepened by the terror on her face.

Semele saw her lover as a god.
Her rash desire was blatant, undenied.
He showed himself, thunder and lightning shod.
Her human eyes were blasted and she died.

And Mary sat, unknowing, unaware.
The angel's wings were wilder than the swan
as God broke through the shining, waiting air,
gave her the lily's sword thrust and was gone.

The swans, the old gods fall in consternation
at the fierce coming of the wild wind's thrust
entering Mary in pure penetration.
The old gods die now, crumbled stone and rust.

Young Mary, moved by Gabriel, acquiesced,
asked nothing for herself in lowliness,
accepted, too, the pain, and then, most blest,
became the bearer of all holiness.

The Bethlehem explosion

And it came to pass in those days that there went out a decree from Caesar Augustus, that all the world should be taxed. And Joseph also went up from Galilee . . . to be taxed, with Mary his espoused wife, being great with child. Luke 2:1, 4-5

The chemistry lab at school
was in an old greenhouse
surrounded by ancient live oaks
garnished with Spanish moss.

The experiment I remember best
was pouring a quart of clear fluid
into a glass jar, and dropping into it,
grain by grain, salt-sized crystals,
until they layered
like white sand on the floor of the jar.

One more grain—and suddenly—
water and crystal burst
into a living, moving pattern,
a silent, quietly violent explosion.
The teacher told us that only when
we supersaturated the solution,
would come the precipitation.

The little town
was like the glass jar in our lab.
One by one they came, grain by grain,
all those of the house of David,
like grains of sand to be counted.

The inn was full. When Joseph knocked,
his wife was already in labour; there was no room
even for compassion. Until the barn was offered.
That was the precipitating factor. A child was born,
and the pattern changed forever, the cosmos
shaken with that silent explosion.

Young Mary

I know not all of that which I contain.
I'm small; I'm young; I fear the pain.
All is surprise: I am to be a mother.
That Holy Thing within me and no other
is Heaven's King whose lovely Love will reign.
My pain, his gaining my eternal gain
my fragile body holds Creation's Light;
its smallness shelters God's unbounded might.
The angel came and gave, did not explain.
I know not all of that which I contain.

Three songs of Mary

1. *O Simplicitas*

An angel came to me
and I was unprepared
to be what God was using.
Mother I was to be.
A moment I despaired,
thought briefly of refusing.
The angel knew I heard.
According to God's Word
I bowed to this strange choosing.

A palace should have been
the birthplace of a king
(I had no way of knowing).
We went to Bethlehem;
it was so strange a thing.
The wind was cold, and blowing,
my cloak was old, and thin.
They turned us from the inn;
the town was overflowing.

God's Word, a child so small
who still must learn to speak
lay in humiliation.
Joseph stood, strong and tall.
The beasts were warm and meek
and moved with hesitation.
The Child born in a stall?

I understood it: all.
Kings came in adoration.

Perhaps it was absurd;
a stable set apart,
the sleepy cattle lowing;
and the incarnate Word
resting against my heart.
My joy was overflowing.
The shepherds came, adored
the folly of the Lord,
wiser than all men's knowing.

2. O Oriens

O come, O come Emmanuel
within this fragile vessel here to dwell.
O Child conceived by heaven's power
give me thy strength: it is the hour.

O come, thou Wisdom from on high;
like any babe at life you cry;
for me, like any mother, birth
was hard, O light of earth.

O come, O come, thou Lord of might,
whose birth came hastily at night,
born in a stable, in blood and pain
is this the king who comes to reign?

O come, thou Rod of Jesse's stem,
the stars will be thy diadem.
How can the infinite finite be?
Why choose, child, to be born of me?

O come, thou key of David, come,
open the door to my heart-home.
I cannot love thee as a king —
so fragile and so small a thing.

O come, thou Day-spring from on high:
I saw the signs that marked the sky.
I heard the beat of angels' wings
I saw the shepherds and the kings.

O come, Desire of nations, be
simply a human child to me.
Let me not weep that you are born.
The night is gone. Now gleams the morn.

Rejoice, rejoice, Emmanuel,
God's Son, God's Self, with us to dwell.

3. O Sapientia

It was from Joseph first I learned
of love. Like me he was dismayed.
How easily he could have turned
me from his house; but, unafraid,
he put me not away from him
(O God-sent angel, pray for him).
Thus through his love was Love obeyed.

The Child's first cry came like a bell:
God's Word aloud, God's Word in deed.
The angel spoke: so it befell,
and Joseph with me in my need.
O Child whose father came from heaven,
to you another gift was given,
your earthly father chosen well.

With Joseph I was always warmed
and cherished. Even in the stable
I knew that I would not be harmed.
And, though above the angels swarmed,
man's love it was that made me able
to bear God's love, wild, formidable,
to bear God's will, through me performed.

O wise and foolish virgins

Her rounded belly moved with life.
He felt it with his calloused hands
the pain slashed through her like a knife.
She fell, gave way to birth's demands,
　　and in her pain
　　delivered Cain.
New life within her body grew.
Trembling, he led her to the stall
and quivered as the pain knifed through.
He thought he heard an angel call.
　　Her flesh was torn—
　　Jesus was born.

Now we await the final birth.
The oil has spilled. No one is wise.
The galaxies and our small earth
labour in pain at time's demise.
　　Like her, I call,
　　Come, Lord of all!

First coming

He did not wait till the world was ready,
till men and nations were at peace.
He came when the Heavens were unsteady,
and prisoners cried out for release.

He did not wait for the perfect time.
He came when the need was deep and great.
He dined with sinners in all their grime,
turned water into wine. He did not wait

till hearts were pure. In joy he came
to a tarnished world of sin and doubt.
To a world like ours, of anguished shame
he came, and his Light would not go out.

He came to a world which did not mesh,
to heal its tangles, shield its scorn.
In the mystery of the Word made Flesh
the Maker of the stars was born.

We cannot wait till the world is sane
to raise our songs with joyful voice,
for to share our grief, to touch our pain,
He came with Love: Rejoice! Rejoice!

After annunciation

This is the irrational season
when love blooms bright and wild.
Had Mary been filled with reason
there'd have been no room for the child.

Like every newborn

The Lord is King, and hath put on glorious appeal; the Lord hath put on his apparel, and girded himself with strength. Psalm 93:1

Like every newborn, he has come from very far.
His eyes are dazzled by the brilliance of the star.
So glorious is he, he goes to this immoderate length
to show his love for us, discarding power and strength.
Girded for war, humility his mighty dress,
He moves into the battle wholly weaponless.

The Wise Men

A star has streaked the sky,
pulls us,
calls.
Where, oh where, where leads the light?

We came and left our gifts
and turned
homeward.
Time had passed, friends gone from sight—

One by one, they go, they die
to now,
to us—
gone in the dazzling dark of night.

Oh how, and where, and when, and why,
and what,
and who,
and may, and should, O God, and might

a star, a wind, a laugh, a cry
still come
from one—
the blazing word of power and might—

to use our gifts of gold and myrrh
and frankincense
as needed,
as our intention was to do the right?

Here, there, hear—soft as a sigh—
willing,
loving
all that is spoken, back to the flight

blazing too fierce for mortal eye.
Renew—
redeem,
oh, Love, until we, too, may dazzle bright.

One king's epiphany

I shall miss the stars.

Not that I shall stop looking
as they pattern their wild wills each night
across an inchoate sky, but I must see them with a different awe.
If I trace their flames' ascending and descending—
relationships and correspondences—
then I deny what they have just revealed.
The sum of their oppositions, juxtapositions,
led me to the end of all sums:
a long journey, cold, dark and uncertain,
toward the ultimate equation.
How can I understand? If I turn back from this,
compelled to seek all answers in the stars,
then this—Who—they have led me to
is not the One they said: they will have lied.
No stars are liars!
My life on their truth!
If they had lied about this
I could never trust their power again.

But I believe they showed the truth,
truth breathing,
truth Whom I have touched with my own hands,
worshipped with my gifts.
If I have bowed, made
obeisance to this final arithmetic,
I cannot ask the future from the stars without betraying
the One whom they have led me to.
It will be hard not to ask, just once again,

to see by mathematical forecast where he will grow,
where go, what kingdom conquer, what crown wear.
But would it not be going beyond truth
(the obscene *reductio ad absurdum*)
to lose my faith in truth once, and once for all
revealed in the full dayspring of the sun?

I cannot go back to night.
O Truth, O small and unexpected thing,
You have taken so much from me.
How can I bear wisdom's pain?
But I have been shown: and I have seen.

Yes. I shall miss the stars.

. . . and kill the Passover   Exodus 12:21

Angel! Messenger of light and death—
Is it by God's will that you have come?
Each year I gave thanks and rejoiced
that the blood of the lamb was on the lintel
and you passed over the homes of Israel,
God's children, and did not put your cold hand
upon our first born babes. It was only those Egyptians,
the babes of those who worshipped foreign gods—
or no gods at all—that you struck down.
I did not even notice
the mourning of those Egyptian mothers.
Was not this God's doing, and for our sakes,
that our people might go free of bondage?
Our mothers held their living infants
to their breasts; perhaps they laughed with joy.
Our God had once more saved his Chosen People.

God!
Was not my slaughtered baby chosen, too?
Who is this child whose stabled birth
caused Herod's panic and revenge? Lord!
Every Hebrew manchild under two, clubbed, stabbed, killed.
Who was your angel, then? Angel of light and death—
was it God's sword that flashed against our babes?
How can I ever again rejoice at Passover,
when other women's babes, innocent of all guile,
were slaughtered by your angel?
Passover—and where's my child—
my Herod-hated, slaughtered, butchered babe?
Your ways are not our ways, O God of love.

64

I do not understand the evil angels sent
among Egyptians, nor the mothers,
bereaved as Rachel, weeping for their dead.
I hold the bloody body of my babe and curse you
that you did not stay the cruel sword.
Is this your love, that all these die
that one star-heralded man-child should live?
And what will be his end, O Lord? How will he die?
How will you show this one saved child your love?

Mary: after the baptism

Yes, of course. On many days I doubted.
My faith grew out of doubt. The child was good
but other babies have been good. He shouted
when he was hungry, like any child, for food.
One simply does not think of the Messiah
cutting teeth, eating, and eliminating.
He springs, full-grown, in the great Isaiah—
God, servant, king. And I was waiting,
remembering in my heart the very things
that caused my doubt: the angel's first appearing
to me and then to Joseph; shepherds, kings,
the flight to Egypt. Remembering was fearing;
doubt helped. I had to face it all as true
the day John baptized him. Then he knew.

The preparation of Mary, mother of Joses

Neither virgin nor wise
I fill foolishly
my lamp, lest surprise
take me unprepared. Mulishly
at mid-morning sun-time
I pour in the oil.
(I'm anticipating as usual.)
Toil is my lot,
my daily drink and meat.
The Bridegroom will find me workworn and rough.
But my lamp is ready, and even as I am,
I'll gladly greet Him who comes.
And that is joy enough.

Andrew

Jesus, too, needed friends; close friends
and solitude. The companionable meal,
laughter and talk—then he, the one who spends
himself must turn himself, turn, and conceal
himself in desert emptiness to be
by Father filled. And then poured strength upon
all the emptiest, the most in need. And he,
being human for us, needed me, Peter and John.
So taught he us. So did we learn
this lovely rhythm—needing, needed—then
the deepest of all needs, the heartward turn
to Love's own source, the spring which fills all men,
Son-lit, Father-filled, Spirit-blown.
By yourself, Lord, to us our self is shown.

The Samaritan woman at the well

The waters are wild, are wild.
Billows batter with unchannelled might.
A turmoil of waves foams on the ocean's face
wind-whipped the waters hurl

the rivers rush

fountains burst from the rocks
the rapids break huge boulders into dust
the skies split with torrential rains

waters meet waters
the wind and waves are too tumultuous
no one can meet them and survive

In this wilderness of water
we shall all be drowned
the ocean cannot be compassed

I weep, I die
Put my tears in your bottle

drowning
I thirst

Look!
the water is in a cup

(O Lord open thou our lips)

I thirst

Is it any less water
because you have contained it for us
in a vessel we can touch?

Song of blind Bartimaeus after his healing

All praise to thee, my God, this night
for all I see, both night and day.
All praise for loveliness of things!

During the shadows of un-sight
you kept the raging fears at bay.
All praise to thee, my God, this night

for all the blessings of the light,
for sand and sun and eagles' wings,
all praise for loveliness of things!

Praise for sandals, garments white,
for children's faces, eyes alight,
all praise to thee, my God, this night.

All praise for butterflies in flight,
for work-worn hands, for golden hay,
the purple shadows evening brings,

for brass and copper polished bright,
for lifting light that shows the way,
all praise to thee, my God, this night,
all praise for loveliness of things!

The woman

Jesus, to the woman taken in adultery: Go, and sin no more.

It is not
what it was
or could have been
or might have been
or should have been
or what I thought it would be
or dreamed about
or expected
or longed for
or prayed for.

It is what is.
Nowhere else but
Here. Now.
Only in the is
(not the ought)
does love grow—
is joy found.

Never in vain hopings
in vanity
in vaunting
or wishing or pretending
or dreaming
but here. Now.

Never in saying
it was not my fault

it shouldn't have been
I couldn't help it
but I meant
but he didn't
but you don't understand.

Never
there.
Only here
in the painful light
of my own sin
accepted
seen in its ugliness
repented
forgiven
(forgiveness hurts)

let me turn
seeking nothing
asking nothing
here
only here
is the longed for
Word.

Only now can I say
I love you.

When Mary asked for him, Jesus said, "Who is my mother? And who are my brethren?" Matthew 12:46-48

He heals, my son, he heals the blind,
the lepers, and those possessed of unclean spirits.
When his hands touch, no wound is mortal.
But we can still die. Day
can be held back by night's uncomprehending portal.

I bleed. I faint. I die.
(A sword will pierce you, Simeon said.)
Nothing is automatic, nothing is guaranteed.
Love is not killed although my heart may cry
as the sword pierces. Love may not heed

betrayal or rejection, being
of its essence impossible, like everything essential.
While love is dying it is being reborn. Seeing
its own mortal wound it is of confidential

opinion that these are pains of labour.
During love's delivery I am ripped and torn.
Who, my son asks, who is your neighbour?
Son, all that matters is that love is born.

The High Priest's servant

Sometimes I take it out and look at it
(unrecognizable now
unless one knew it full of blood and sound)
shrivelled like an old heel of bread,
or piece of fungus.

I was certainly not prepared.
I knew my master had it in for
some itinerant preacher,
and it seemed to me that his high priest's fear and anger
exceeded anything this Galilean might do.
But my master was always given to extremes,
and what could I do but go along
with him and the others
on that warm, crucial night?

It would have been simpler
to take the man by day (though less dramatic).
We came to the agreed-on place,
where an ill-named friend approached to kiss him
so we'd be certain we had the right man.
After a sudden flurry of torches and shouting
a stunning pain slashed down my head.
The roar of anguish within me
was louder than my scream.

And then he touched me, this strange man we'd trapped,
and the intolerable roaring cleared,
and I heard the small song of a night bird,

and the wind moving in the olive trees
beyond the heavy breathing of frightened men.

I bent down and picked it up.
Then lifted my hands,
felt my head, and two ears, warm and hearing.

And my life was shattered, turned around,
and changed forever. I left the high priest,
never to return.

There is danger now.
Often we do not understand
our freedom, and the fresh blood flowing in our lives.
That is why I sometimes take it out and look at it,
unrecognizable now,
unless one knew it full of song and sound.

Andrew: having run away from Jesus in the garden

Who is this stranger who I hardly know,
(despite his presence within me) who cannot
be kept decently silent and unseen
(Lord, I still feel my muscles, tight from running),
with whom I must be reconciled
before I can sleep? This unwelcome
intruder who is my self
must be forgiven and accepted
and somehow loved. You have forgiven me,
with your unexpected presence among us.
But even in my joy I know I betrayed you
and must forever know that this coward, too,
is as much me as the loyal disciple I thought to be.

This stranger who is most of me is still
my Lord's failed friend, but friend nevertheless,
and in this friend I now must find, before I sleep,
His image, and His love.

Magdalen

I sold that which is forever and unspeakably priceless.
I was paid for that which can only be given away.
Asked for my reasons I stood, strangely struck voiceless.
A cloud unexpectedly darkened the brilliant day.

I turned from the cushions, the perfumes, the endless lying.
Hunger meant nothing; I was replete at last.
I think I was born, yet I know that this is dying.
I eat of the feast as I turn away for the fast.

In fear, in joy, I lose myself in the finding.
The lusts of the body are shriven, the flesh is new.
Fresh grave cloths are all my selfish self is binding.
Lord! This is my body which I would give for you.

Mary of Magdala

How do I find You, who have been blinded by
    the brilliance of your Father?
The darkness is heavy in tangible weight.
Am I afraid of light? Would I rather
remain in the shadows, afraid of the brightness
    of your face?
Why must I stay here where the black clouds gather,
trying to slow the hours in this dim place,
to halt time's vast, inexorable race.

How do I find You? Through what graces?
Why am I frightened by the height
    of this wild, windy day
I who have always passionately loved light?
Why do I see you in the darkest places,
touch your garment only when I turn away?
Or see your radiance when ugliness and grief
seem to leave no room for you to stay?
I see you in distorted, hungry faces.
In crusts and filthy gutters is belief
in your love breaking all hate.
You have left your traces
on this demoniac's freed face and joy-streaked cheek.

I find you, Lord, when I no longer clutch.
I find you when I learn to let you go,
and then you reach out with your healing touch.
Seven demons left my tortured mind!
My Lord, so stern, so infinitely kind,
I know myself at last becaue *you* know.

Temper my intemperance

Temper my intemperance, O Lord,
O hallowed, O adored,
my heart's creator, mighty, wild,
temper thy untempered child.
Blaze my eye and blast my ear,
let me never fear to fear,
nor forget what I have heard,
even your voice, my Lord.
Even your Word.

Simon of Cyrene

I've rolled too many stones—nay, boulders—
up this never-ending hill, pushing my shoulders
against the heavy, jagged chunk of granite,
crying against the weight of the entire planet,
staggering like one condemned, up, up the mountain,
the long road dusty, never a spring or fountain,
pushing this boulder which grows heavier steadily,
the Eumenides at my heels, implacable, deadly.
If I near the top, the rock's at the bottom again.
There's no end to labour, climbing, struggle, pain.

Who do you think you are, carrying another man's stone?
Sisyphus is gone long since; the old gods gone.
Other men's burdens are not your burden unless
they're offered you freely, never under duress.
What you must carry was long ago prepared
before the morning stars sang and the worlds were shared.
Its weight is infinite; yet you will find it light.
It will bow your back, and yet you must walk upright.
The hill is endless, but you will reach its peak.
The strong will falter; help will come from the weak.
When you have reached the place where others before you have stood,
you will find that your burden is made not of stone, but of wood.

Barabbas

Son of man
Son of the Father—
who can
tell one from the other?
Son of man
must taste of death.
Father's son,
I would rather
be the one
to return
to Father's side
than to remain
to mourn
man's son's pain.
So he died
while my breath
burned in the rain.

Son of man
dead for me,
crucified,
to set me free.
Son of the Father,
I must be
because my brother
toppled death
upon a tree.

The cross's death
becomes life's door.

Son of man
offers more
abundant life
than those whose scorn
had thought to kill
the coming morn.

Son of man
my life will turn,
as to our Father
I return.

Mary speaks:

O you who bear the pain of the whole earth,
　　I bore you.
O you whose tears give human tears their worth,
　　I laughed with you.
You, who, when your hem is touched, give power,
　　I nourished you.
Who turn the day to night in this dark hour,
　　light comes from you.
O you who hold the world in your embrace,
　　I carried you.
Whose arms encircled the world with your grace,
　　I once held you.
O you who laughed and ate and walked the shore,
　　I played with you.
And I, who with all others, you died for,
　　now I hold you.

May I be faithful to this final test:
in this last time I hold my child, my son,
his body close enfolded to my breast,
the holder held: the bearer borne.
Mourning to joy: darkness to morn.
Open, my arms: your work is done.

Salome: at the foot of the cross   Mark 15:40

It is the crossbeam with its earthbound weight,
that hurts, that makes his uphill road unending.
At the summit the upright waits, uncompromising, unbending.
He will have unthinkable pain, perhaps no angels tending,
so solitary is the road, so strait the gate.

Does this road go uphill only?
Is death all that waits at the end?

Under the cross I sit and, time-bound, wait
for time to fit the crossbeam to the upright, knowing
the end. He staggers, he is here, his weakness growing.
Flesh and wood shudder under the icy blowing.
Oh, Lord, is this how all our hopes must end?

Pushing through dark, in fiercest concentration,
it is now, as he stands beneath the crossbeam's weight
that he strengthens, stretches, now he carries nothing,
it would seem, except himself. It is too late
for me to bear it for him, carry his beam,
and not the beam in my own eye, blinding, blowing.
Oh, God, the hammer, the nails. Lord.

He is stretched out, his strong arms
nailed to the crossbeam,
his dust-darkened feet to the upright.

Is there only time, this sky-darkened time?
As night dies to morning,
will his dawn ever break again?

Three days

Friday:

When you agree to be the mother of God
you make no conditions, no stipulations.
You flinch before neither cruel thorn nor rod.
You accept the tears; you endure the tribulations.

But, my God, I didn't know it would be like this.
I didn't ask for a child so different from others.
I wanted only the ordinary bliss,
to be the most mundane of mothers.

Saturday:

When I first saw the mystery of the Word
made flesh I never thought that in his side
I'd see the callous wound of Roman sword
piercing my heart on the hill where he died.

How can the Word be silenced? Where has it gone?
Where are the angel voices that sang at his birth?
My frail heart falters. I need the light of the Son.
What is this darkness over the face of the earth?

Sunday:

Dear God, He has come, the Word has come again.
There is no terror left in silence, in clouds, in gloom.
He has conquered the hate; he has overcome the pain.
Where, days ago, was death lies only an empty tomb.

The secret should have come to me with his birth,
when glory shone through darkness, peace through strife.
For every birth follows a kind of death,
and only after pain comes life.

Pieta

The other Marys radiated joy.
The disciples found the truth hard to believe.
There had to be breaking bread, eating fish,
before they, too, even Thomas, were lit with joyfulness.

Not much was said about me.
I said good-bye to the son I carried within me
for nine months, nursed, fed, taught to walk.
On Friday when they took him down from the cross,
I held the son I knew,
recognizing him in my arms,
and never saw him again,
not my body's child.

How could I laugh, weep tears of joy?
Like the others, I failed to recognize him;
the Christ who rose was not Bethlehem's babe.
And it was right. For this was meant to be.
Here in my head I would not have had it otherwise.
But empty arms still longed for familiar flesh.
My joy, a sword that pierced through my heart.

I understood, more, perhaps, than the others
when he said that he could not stay with us—
that it was better if he went away,
was one again with God, his Father.

And when the Spirit came
I once again could love my son
and know my Lord.

If Easter came later for me than for the others,
its brilliance was as poignant and bright.

Mary: afterwards

John. John, can you not take me to him,
you who were more than friend, who are now my son?
After all we have known and borne together
can you deny to me now that you've surely seen him?
Can you conceal his whereabouts from his mother?
I ran to the place where the other Marys knew him;
I saw the empty tomb, the enormous stone
rolled from its mouth, the grave clothes lying.
I called, I cried, with no one there to hear me.
Joy and grief raged in my longing heart.
He was not there, nor even the flaming angel.
I was the last to be told. Why were you all
afraid to say what I most wanted to hear?
I know: the Magdalen said that she couldn't touch him,
that she knew him only because he called her: Mary!
On the Emmaus road they didn't know they'd been walking
beside him until he was known in the breaking of bread.
John, do you fear that perhaps I wouldn't know him?
Perhaps it would give me pain to find my son
so changed from the son I knew, the son I circled
first with my body, last with my anguished arms.

John: I can bear to know that I may not hold him.
The angel who came to me once will help me now.
I don't need to touch him. Just let me see him . . .
Don't be impatient: "Mother, you don't understand!"
I've never pretended, my dear, to understand him.
Only to love him, to be there if ever he needed
to know I was by him, waiting and loving—
Oh, John. Yes. I see. That's how it will be, then?

You don't know where he is? You're alone, and then
he's with you, but it's different now.
He comes, and he's gone, and you know him
only by what he says or what he does,
by his hands and feet, or in the breaking of bread.
The angel told me before his birth, and Simeon
after, and I haven't ever asked more—or less.
If my joy in him must rest only in your witness
that he is risen, that he is risen indeed,
then he has given you to me to help me bear it.
We have shared the cup, and the dark of night is done.
I will know my son through you he has given me for my son.

Thomas: after seeing the wounds

As you depended from a tree,
so depend I, Lord, on thee.
Thou my cross; on thee impaled
is my body. Now I see
how our hands and feet are nailed,

nailed by joy and nailed by pain:
strength of thine own scars remain.
Thou the cross from dark to sun,
stretching boughs to wind and rain,
upholding all, witholding none.

Lord, on thee do I depend.
Thy limbs hold me, heal me, mend
all unbelieving doubts. And now
I do not break, I bend, I bend:
thou hast made of me a bough.

As thou depended from a tree
so depend I, Lord, on thee.
Of thy body made a part
I was blind, and now I see:
all life and love are because thou art.

Peter

Lord, I love you.
I have tried to feed your sheep.
Shepherds have a lonely job.

I have gone out searching for you
into the tumult of the midnight sky—
the swirling life of stars too many to count,
and have been deafened
by the rush of the wind.
And now you ask me to look within,
away from the vast and echoing sound without.

So I go down and in,
into the deepest, narrowest,
darkest, most brilliant
places of the heart.
I am battered by its beat
throbbing in my veins,
tension, release.
In the small space
between the beats,
the rhythm
yours, not mine,
yours is its time
to keep me here, in time,
in, deeper, deeper,
to the beating of my heart

So I end where I began
and once again I start
to learn that my disgrace
is ripped, is torn apart,
and mended by your grace.

A man from Phrygia, on Pentecost

Lord, I did not choose to be comforted.
I am not ready to bear the many things
you have yet to say: you said it yourself.
But you have sent me (against my will) your comforter
and what is comfort but an iron command?

I don't want to obey. I won't. Yes: I will.
Why must I interrupt my self-indulgent weakness
to respond to the austerity of your demand?
I must set my face sternly towards truth
as you turned toward Jerusalem, that all
obedience should be shown us and accomplished.
Your way to truth is hard, is dark, is pain.
You have shown me the way, O Lord, but I
am not prepared to bear your comfort.
And yet, unwilling, unready, recalcitrant,
I receive the flaming thrust that you have sent,
and voices speaking as in my own tongue,
and nothing will ever be the same again.

Barnabas, travelling to Antioch

The road is long, my friend,
and not smooth. We expected
the dark forest, the thorns,
and unsuspected pitfalls.
We even knew that some
would turn away from us, toward
broader, easier roads. It hurt,
but did not surprise,
when they denied the way and placed traps
for the pilgrims. The sharp iron teeth
snapped shut, broke bone, made much blood.
And so we walked, dragging the brokenness.
Pain became a constant companion,
relieved only by laughter
and the breaking of bread.
In the darkness we sometimes hurt each other
and did not even know what we had done.

The road is long, my friend,
and the journey rough.
This harsh wood
prepared for each one on this path
grows heavy by afternoon.

There's not much rest.
We walk as strangers in this foreign land with no rest
and yet this uphill road leads to the light of home.
The night is far spent. The day is at hand.

Phoebe, perhaps the very first deacon

Quoniam tu illuminas lucernam meam Domine: Deus meus illumina tenebras meas.

There was fire in the bush when Moses first
spoke with God.
There was light too brilliant to be borne.
God covered the prophet's eyes with his hand.
And then in the darkness they talked.
Beyond sight, Moses heard
and listened to the Word.

But I am like a child at bedtime,
frightened of the dark,
crying out for a drink of water
that the door may open,
crying for water
but thirsty for light.

I must leave Egypt and follow the cloud,
for only in that place beyond the galaxies,
further than starfire and the blaze of suns,
only beyond all light, beyond all hope of human sight
will I see the source of all illumination
in the radiant glory of the Word.

But I am like a child in a strange house at night
groping through shadowy rooms
toward the sound of voices,
afraid to call and ask where the light can be found.

Further than any man can go alone.
in the deepest, darkest reaches of the heart:
here the light is lit, the invisible light
by which alone we see.

Come light this tiny candle, Lord.
Give me a flame of understanding according to your Word.

Priscilla's response to the letter to the Hebrews

He is
the Word
Creator
he who shall be at the end
the glory
face of God
the cleanser, sin destroyer
the Visitor.

He is not
an angel, for he names them
and they worship him.

He will never
change or disappear
though he makes change
and will be at the end and beyond.

He is
greater than the angels
Son of the Father
the just ruler
the chosen one
the joyful.

He is
in Time
lower than the angels
perfect through suffering
our brother
the death destroyer.

He is not
an angel, for he knows death

and when he died,
so did death.

and so
He is
our helper in temptation.

He is not
untempted.

He is
our high priest
faithful in all things.

He is not
stubborn, as we are,
rebellious and tempting.

He is
our rest
and our Way of rest.

He is
the sword that cuts us open
exposing us to the Father.

He is
weak for our sakes

called to be our high priest.

He is
obedient unto death.

He is
the promiser
the keeper of the promise
the promise itself.

He is
the king of righteousness
the Prince of Peace
the blesser
and the blessing.

He does not
hear and refuse to believe.

He is not
indifferent to our weakness
unsympathetic to our pain
ungentle with our weakness.

He does not
choose himself but he is chosen.

He is not
a child like us, who must be
children before he can grow us up.
He will never
forget, nor be unfair, nor
impatient with our impatience.

He does not
collect from us one-tenth
but all.

He is not
so much the collector as
the collected.
He is not
the law, but the changer of the law.

He is
wholly different
the power of life which has no
    end.
He is
the one once sacrifice
high priest in the tent God
        pitched among us
the real pattern.

He is not
temporal power, or the old
covenant, which was in time.
    He does not
pass on to others his work as priest
or offer daily sacrifice.
    He is not
the shadow but the caster of
    shadow.
    He does not
write his law on stone but in our
    hearts.

He is
the true testator
by the shedding of blood.

He pours
out his own blood to drown our
    sins.
    He is
the end of the old sacrifices
the one forever sacrifice for sin
who with the sacrifice is
    perfecter.

Not
the blood of goats or calves
        but his own.
    He is not
a copy of the original
repeating over and over

offering over and over what he
has offered once and forever.

He is
freedom from the law.

He is not
the law.

He is
the way of truth, judge and fire
terrible
living God.

He is
who came
who will come.
He is
that which can be seen
from that which cannot be seen.
He
makes the world
condemns the world
redeems the world.

He is
the weak who is all strength
the dying who raises from the
    dead
who dies and rose
and sits at the right hand of
    God.
He is
the Son who suffered that we
    might become sons.

He is not
the possible but the impossible
leaving his own country
without knowing where he was
    going
and living with us as a
stranger in a strange land.

He did not
think back to the country he had.
He is not
Abraham but Isaac
not Isaac but the ram caught in
    the burning bush.

He is not
obedient to the law but to God.

He is
He who speaks.

He is
the divine message
the earth shaker
destroying fire
destroying fear
unending
unchangeable
death dying
life raising.

He is
the glory forever and ever.

He is not
held in by any walls
but dies outside the gate
that we might follow him
leaving the temporal city
to share his shame
and so see the city
which is to come.

Amen   Amen   Amen

Mary speaks: from Ephesus

Now that I have spent these years in this strange place
of luminous stone and golden light and dying gods,
now that I have listened to the wild music
of given-son, John, I begin to understand.

In the beginning I was confused and dazzled;
a plain girl, unused to angels.
Then there was the hard journey to Bethlehem,
and the desperate search for a place to stay,
my distended belly ripe and ready for deliverance.
In the dark of the cave, night air sweet with the moist breath
of domestic beasts, I laughed, despite my pains,
at their concern. Joseph feared that they would frighten me
with their anxious stampings and snortings,
but their anxiety was only for me, and not because of me.
One old cow, udder permanently drooping,
mooed so with my every contracting
that my birthing-cries could not be heard.
And so my baby came with pain and tears and much hilarity.

Afterwards, swaddled and clean, he was so small and tender
that I could not think beyond my present loving
to all this strange night pointed. The shepherds came
clumsily gruff and knelt, and brought their gifts,
and, later on, the kings; and all I knew was marvel.
His childhood was sheer joy to me. He was merry and loving,
moved swiftly from laughter to long, unchildlike silences.
The years before his death were bitter for me.
I did not understand, and sometimes thought that it was he
who had lost comprehension of the promise of his birth.

His death was horrible. But now I understand
that death was not his sacrifice, but birth.
It was not the cross which was his sacrifice.
It was his birth which must have been, for him,
most terrible of all. Think. If I were to be born
out of compassion, as one of the small wood-lice
in the door-sill of our hut, limit myself to the comprehension
of those small dark creatures, unable to know sea or sun or song
or John's bright words, to live and die thus utterly restricted,
it would be nothing, nothing to the radiant Word
coming to dwell, for man, in man's confined and cabined flesh.

This was the sacrifice, this ultimate gift of love.
I thought once that I loved. My love was hundredfold less
than his, than the love of the wood-lice is to mine,
and even this I do not know. For has he not, or will he not
come to the wood-lice as he came to man? Does he not
give his own self to the lowing cattle, the ear of corn,
the blazing sun, the clarion moon, the drop of rain?
His compassion is infinite, his sacrifice incomprehensible,
breaking through the darkness of our loving-lack.

Oh, my son, who was and is and will be, my night draws close.
Come, true light, which taketh away the sin of the world,
and bring me home. My hour is come. Amen.

Ephesus

They walked these self-same stones.
Mary was wilting, weary with the journey,
weary with the years and all that she
had understood and had not understood.
Obedient always, she deferred to John,
smiling a mother's smile at his great joy.
Chariots of gold raced through the godless streets;
Apollo and Diana had grown dim;
only the emperor was god.
They paused, perhaps, Mary and John,
at these same vacant gates
of the sad temple of forgotten gods,
and Mary smiled and turned and said,
"My son, the old gods have been lost."
And John replied, "Bring we now the new—"

And in his harrowing of a shadowed Hell
perhaps the old gods were redeemed as well,
and joyfully sing their praise to him
with cherubim and seraphim.

Mary Magdalene, remembering:

All time is holy.
We move through the dark
following his footprints by touch.
He walked the lonesome valley.
His time is holy.

We will break bread together.
We will move through the dark.
He has gone away from us.
The wine is poured out.
We will eat broken bread.

That Friday was good.
We will move through the dark.
Death died on Friday.
The blood-stained cross bore hope.
His Friday is good.

We will hold hands
as we move through the dark.
Saturday he walked through hell,
making all things new.
We will hold hands.

This is the meaning
of our walk through the dark.
Love's light will lead us
through the stone at the tomb.
He is the meaning.

He called me by name
as I stood in the dark.
Suddenly I knew him.
He came. Then he left us,
he will come again.

And Nicolas a proselyte of Antioch, who, they set before the apostles: and when they had prayed, they laid their hands on them, and the word of God increased. Acts 6:5-7

I don't understand, dear God.
Do you do it just to make us face
our abominable pride,
to prove to us what needs proving
over and over again:
that of ourselves we are nothing,
and then you take this nothing
that you have made from nothing
and use it to your own good purpose?

But why, Lord?
Surely there are people you could use
who are better than we,
either the old Israel or the new?
We don't flatter ourselves (do we?)
that we are the only ones you can choose
(circumcised or uncircumcised
always stiff-necked).

And then, it's not just your choice of a nation
or of those of us who are the dogs
who lick the crumbs from under your table,
but—O Lord, why, for instance, Abraham?
All those wiles and guiles which really weren't honest,
pretending before kings that his wife was his sister
because he was afraid? And we can't make believe
that Jacob's treatment and trickery of Esau
was anything but the kind of thing applauded

by the wily Romans who consider it smart
to step on your brother's hairy body
to get to the top of the ladder, angels or no.

And yet you chose those devious men.
To us it's irrational and arbitrary, the things you do
over and over again. You burst,
with cloud of your glory,
upon an arrogant tent-maker who would have
nailed you to the cross personally
if he had been on that hill top,
and failing that, delighted in seeing Christians
stoned to bloody, brutal death.
Could you not find even the ten just men
for whom to spare the city?

Why Abraham, why Jacob, why Saul, why me?
Come, then, Lord, as you have always done
to the unjust, the unjustified, the foolish.
Use us despite ourselves
whether we recognize you or not,
whether or not we see that the stumbling block
which you have laid before your people
is the cornerstone of the house.

You come to us, the hopelessly impenitent,
that to your purposes our rude wills may be bent.

Books in the **WHEATON LITERARY** SERIES:

And It Was Good: Reflections on Beginnings, by Madeleine L'Engle. Cloth, 216 pages.

At a Theater Near You: Screen Entertainment from a Christian Perpective, by Thomas Patterson. Trade paper, 216 pages.

The Heart of George MacDonald: A One-Volume Collection of His Most Important Fiction, Essays, Sermons, Drama, and Biographical Information, edited by Rolland Hein. Cloth, 448 pages.

How to Read Slowly: Reading for Comprehension, by James W. Sire. Trade paper, 192 pages.

The Liberated Imagination: Thinking Christianly about the Arts, by Leland Ryken. Trade paper, 283 pages.

Life Essential: The Hope of the Gospel, by George MacDonald, edited by Rolland Hein. Trade paper, 104 pages.

Love Letters, adult fiction by Madeleine L'Engle. Cloth, 304 pages.

Maker & Craftsman: The Story of Dorothy L. Sayers, by Alzina Stone Dale. Trade paper, 172 pages.

Odd Angles of Heaven: Contemporary Poetry by People of Faith, edited by David Craig and Janet McCann. Cloth, 336 pages.

Orthodoxy, by G. K. Chesterton. Cloth, 188 pages.

The Other Side of the Sun, adult fiction by Madeleine L'Engle. Cloth, 384 pages.

Penguins and Golden Calves: Icons and Idols by Madeleine L'Engle. Cloth, 192 pages.

Polishing the Petoskey Stone, poems by Luci Shaw (compiled from **Listen to the Green, The Secret Trees, The Sighting,** and **Postcard from the Shore).** Cloth, 276 pages.

Postcard from the Shore, poems by Luci Shaw. Trade paper, 95 pages.

Realms of Gold: The Classics in Christian Perspective, by Leland Ryken. Trade paper, 240 pages.

The Rock that Is Higher: Story as Truth, by Madeleine L'Engle. Cloth, 296 pages.

The Sighting, poems by Luci Shaw. Trade paper, 95 pages.

Sold into Egypt: Joseph's Journey into Human Being, by Madeleine L'Engle. Cloth, 240 pages.

A Stone for a Pillow: Journeys with Jacob, by Madeleine L'Engle. Cloth, 240 pages.

T. S. Eliot: The Philosopher Poet, by Alzina Stone Dale. Cloth, 209 pages.

Walking on Water: Reflections on Faith and Art, by Madeleine L'Engle. Trade paper, 198 pages.

The Weather of the Heart, poems by Madeleine L'Engle. Trade paper, 96 pages.

WinterSong: Christmas Readings, by Madeleine L'Engle and Luci Shaw. Cloth, 208 pages.

All available from your local bookstore or from Harold Shaw Publishers, Box 567, Wheaton, IL 60189, 1-800-SHAWPUB